AF267580

THE PATHFINDERS PLAYBOOK

Copyright © 2026 Michael Ball

All rights reserved. No part of this publication may be reproduced, distributed, or transmitted in any form or by any means, including photocopying, recording, or other electronic or mechanical methods, without the prior written permission of the publisher, except in the case of brief quotations embodied in critical reviews and certain other non-commercial uses permitted by copyright law.

(✳) **green**hill

https://greenhillpublishing.com.au/

Ball, Michael (author)
bravozulubookhouse.com.au

The Pathfinders Playbook
ISBN 978-1-7637191-4-9 (paperback)
ISBN 978-1-7637191-5-6 (eBook)
SELF-HELP

Typesetting Calluna Regular 11/18pt
Cover Image by Yiran Li (Freepik Image)
Cover and book design by Green Hill Publishing

THE PATHFINDERS PLAYBOOK

How to make the decisions that shape you

MICHAEL BALL

*greenhill

Most people don't fail because they lack intelligence. They don't even fail because they're lazy. Most people fail because they didn't know what they were trying to achieve in the first place and they were trying to do too much at once.

My name is Michael Ball. I spent 11 years working in intelligence in the Royal Australian Air Force where I sat countless missions, worked in operations rooms across the world, and supported assets on a daily basis. I learned to prioritise, analyse and execute through trial and error in one of the most complex and intense environments on Earth.

This book exists so you don't have to walk that path.

I wrote it to help you make decisions, and know why you made them.

And most importantly, I wrote it to help you achieve the things you want to do most in the world.

When the best militaries in the world march to war, they follow a meticulously planned campaign which has been refined for years through something called the **targeting cycle**. This is a war plan that designates critical locations to capture or defend, where to deploy troops and how many, logistics, communications plans, and everything else you can think of. Probably more.

Yet when you are asked at school what you want to do in life, you are given nothing to help you answer the question.

This is one of the biggest decisions you will ever make, and the choice comes to you in Year Nine.

Year Nine is the last time school tells you exactly what to study. After that, your grades determine what you are *allowed* to do next. Subjects you take in Year

Ten limit what you can do in Year Eleven, and then Year Eleven does the same for Year Twelve.

If you complete Year Twelve, you are asked what profession you want to pursue and which university you want to go to. You fire out your grades with a cover letter to all the universities you are interested in, and wait for a reply.

You either get what you want, or you don't, then boom... Before you are even an adult, you have decided what you are going to do for the next decade!

This book points the targeting cycle at you, instead of an enemy country, so that you can identify what you want to do in life and how to get there.

I did not go to university. I did not finish Year Twelve.

There were so many options for me. Should I go full-time at Bunnings? Find an apprenticeship as a mechanic or an electrician? Take another test and go to university?

I was swamped with options and I couldn't decide. So I applied to join the military. After the initial session, I was told I could do any job in the Defence Force. But luckily, I'd had a knee reconstruction and I was colour-blind. These two facts reduced all my job options to just five.

They were: steward, cook, logistics, linguist or intelligence analyst. For me, the choice out of those options was easy.

I chose to be an intelligence analyst in the RAAF, and a week later I started my career in the Australian Defence Force.

The best thing about the military? They remove choice wherever possible. I didn't choose when to eat, what to eat, when to wake up, what to wear, or what I was doing that day. I showed up on time and did what I was told. This formed the first two years of my career in the military.

There were only two streams in my career – RADARs or technical signals. I wasn't even able to choose which one I preferred. This allowed me to focus on the thing in front of me, which was to learn the basics of Signals Intelligence.

After training I was posted to my first unit. I walked in highly confident in my abilities and ready to participate in the fight. But the first time I looked at the campaign map for Iraq, I was overwhelmed by the sheer amount of information. I stared open-mouthed at the map and wondered how anyone could decide to do anything with the huge number of choices before me.

This is where I had my first exposure to **targets**.

target is something that has been assessed as a critical resource for a campaign, and must either be captured, compromised or destroyed.

There's an endless number of targets in any war, and they are added and removed as things change diplomatically, or physically on the ground. For instance, there may be hundreds of targets in a base, but if the base is captured they are no longer valid targets.

In much the same way, we are exposed to countless targets in our lives. This leads me to the first step in the **Pathfinders Playbook.**

Write down every single thing you have ever wanted to do. This can range from climbing Mount Everest to finishing the Harry Potter book series. These are your targets and they will be referred to as goals from now on.

Here is a non-exhaustive list of mine:

- Read all of the Greek classics
- Deadlift 200kgs
- Swim the English Channel
- Become an engineer
- Write a book
- Learn to fly a helicopter
- Build a house from scratch
- Start a small farm
- Be a great father
- Be a great husband
- Climb Mount Everest

Like me, if you really get down to it you can probably come up with about a hundred different things. I have only listed 11 for the sake of a low word count and to keep you interested.

Now, sort them.

As you list them, themes will appear:

Academic

- Read all the Greek classics
- Become an engineer
- Write a book

Physical

- Deadlift 200kg
- Swim the English Channel
- Climb Mount Everest

New Skills

- Learn to fly a helicopter
- Build a house from scratch
- Start a small farm

Family

- Be a great husband
- Be a great father

You can see that I have a focus on physical feats of strength and endurance, learning new skills, my family, and improving my knowledge. Even without adding the rest of my goals, the themes are starting to arise.

Now you know what you are interested in. So what? Well, now you need to focus.

ACTION

Write your goals on the following pages.

Write Your Goals Here

Write Your Goals Here

Targets by themselves are useless.

Let me give you a military example.

In war, every single soldier is a legitimate target. But to remove every single soldier from an army is almost impossible, and very costly to achieve.

So if there are endless targets, how do militaries plan a campaign?

Allow me to introduce you to the concept of **Centres of Gravity**.

A Centre of Gravity (COG) is something that, if removed, will see the opposing military crumble. COGs can be many different things, depending on the specific country involved. It could be a leader, communications, a type of resource...

In this example, we will use fuel. If fuel is removed from the equation, cars and tanks won't drive, planes won't fly and ships won't sail. Fuel is a COG worth pursuing because, if it is removed, the military grinds to a halt.

This can be achieved in many different ways. If the country has no access to their own fuel, diplomatic force could stop imports of fuel to the country; jets or missiles could strike oil refineries and fuel tanks; or covert assets could poison the fuel stores.

There are multiple ways to achieve the same send. The important thing is that the target was identified as a COG and was then pursued relentlessly until success was achieved.

H ow do you identify a COG?

Go back to your goals.

Academic

- Read all the classics
- Become an engineer
- Write a book

Physical

- Deadlift 200kg
- Swim the English Channel
- Climb Mount Everest

New Skills

- Learn to fly a helicopter
- Build a house from scratch
- Start a small farm

Family

✏ Be a great husband

✏ Be a great father

Choose which of your many goals are your most important.

I blended "Be a great husband" and "Be a great father" into my first goal. Then I listed "Write a book" and "Deadlift 200kg".

The average person can pursue about three COGs at once. Any more and they start to split their time too much.

Note that *you should only pick one from a theme. Having more than one from the same theme will split your time and effort on both of the COGs, and cause you to fail.*

ACTION

Select three goals from your list and write them on the following pages of paper labelled **COG***.*

If you can't decide from your list, consult with your friends and family or anyone else that knows you well.

Ensure that at least one COG will take longer than 12 months to achieve, and one can be achieved within 3 months.

Write Your COG 1 Here

Write Your COG 2 Here

Write Your COG 3 Here

In order to achieve a COG, you must work with the end in mind. You already know the state you want to be in – this is your COG. Now you must envision what it will take to get there.

In the example of fuel earlier, I provided three ways to eliminate it from an army. This time we will look at the specific example of using a missile to destroy a fuel tank.

First of all, we need to know where the fuel is. Then we need to know how far our missile can travel. In this instance I will say 300 kilometres. Then we need to identify places it can launch from. Are there any islands within 300 kilometres?

Now I know what I need to use and where I need to use it from. But how do I get it there? This system is too big for a plane so we will need to take it there via ship, which will take five days. The closest port is 2,000 kilometres away.

But the missile system itself is 500 kilometres from the port, so first we must move it up there, and this will take two days.

After some very minimal thinking, we have identified what we are going to use, where we are going to use it, and how long will to take to get it from where it is to where it needs to be.

This is the hidden power of starting at the end and working back to the start. If I had simply listed every single missile in the enemy country and their bases, I would have been swamped with targets and possible ports. But by identifying the closest island and then identifying the only missile capable of shooting that far, I do not need to look at the other missiles at all.

My three COGs were:

- Be a good father and husband
- Deadlift 200kg
- Write a book.

The first one is too personal for a book, the second is too linear. So I shall use the third to show you the process of planning.

This is your first opportunity to analyse the COG and see if it's what you really want, or if you just like the idea of doing it. When I reached this stage, I realised I actually wanted to publish a book, not just write one. This added several significant steps to the process.

The process was still the same. I started with the end in mind:

- Publish a book
- Write a book
- Have an idea.

At this point, I realised I had no idea what it took to publish a book. So I sat in front of a computer and did some research, again starting with the end of the process:

- Publish a book
- Typesetting
- Formatting
- Editing
- Cover design
- Get signed by publisher
- Get signed by an agent
- Find an agent
- Write a book
- Have an idea.

This looked like a better list, but it still seemed too short for such a large task. I thought something as large and complex as a book should have many steps. So I did what I always do when I run into something I didn't understand.

I found a mentor.

My mentor was Nan Berrett, a wonderful woman who gave me her time and attention whenever I needed it. She explained the ins and outs of publishing, and introduced me to the concept of self-publishing.

Under her guidance, I broke my list into this:

- Market the book
- Release the book
- Understand IngramSpark
- Understand Kindle Direct Publishing
- Advanced Review Copies
- Publish the book
- Typesetting
- Formatting
- Proofreading
- Copy editing
- Line editing

- Developmental editing
- Self-editing
- Cover design
- Author webpage
- Email list tool
- Find a small press
- Alpha readers
- Write the book
- Have an idea.

This is a more comprehensive list, and I could not have done it on my own.

It is **always** a good idea to find someone who has done, or works in, the COG you are trying to achieve. They will know what it takes, and they will be able to get you there faster than you ever could on your own.

ACTION

Pick one COG from your list and write down exactly what it looks like when it's complete.

Then list the step before that stage.

Then the step before that one, and so on.

Keep going until you reach where you are now.

BONUS ACTION

Identify a mentor who has done what you are trying to do. Reach out to them and see if they are willing to help you follow in their footsteps.

Write Your COG 1 Plan Here

Write the name of your mentor:

Write Your COG 2 Plan Here

Write the name of your mentor:

Write Your COG 3 Plan Here

Write the name of your mentor:

Now, if every goal you broke down into a list was achieved, the world would be a very organised place filled with exceptional people. But the reality is that most of us get drawn away from our hyper-organised list of goals by the constant barrage of distractions in our lives.

The good thing is, I am not here to lecture you about your Facebook usage, or your Instagram/TikTok doom scrolling. These are time sinks, but they aren't what truly stop you from achieving a COG. If you have streamlined your goals to COGs, the limited time you have left after your daily dose of social media lets you chip away at them.

The thing that **will** pull you away from achieving your COGs, is the list of all those other goals you identified at the beginning of the process. They will pull you in multiple directions, and the time you have left will be split between them. But if you try to do everything, you will finish nothing.

Only by **actively ignoring** those other goals, will you be able to achieve the ones you have chosen as most important.

This is crucial.

It is the absolute hardest thing to do in the whole framework. The goals are listed because they mean something to you. It is easy to ignore quantum physics if you have no wish to learn it; however, it requires discipline and a relentless, focused mindset to only work towards the goals you have chosen.

If you want to win, you have to focus your time and energy.

One of the wonderful things about planning is that it shows you choices that you need to make.

For example, if your COG requires landing thousands of troops on the enemy's land, you had better find a way of dealing with anti-ship and anti-air missiles.

The same goes for our COGs. If we take my list from the previous chapter, you may notice there are a few significant but hidden choices among the steps to publishing my book.

Engaging a small press, creating an author page, several rounds of editing, cover design, typesetting, formatting and marketing, all require money.

How much is this going to cost? How long is it going to take?

All up, I spent about $15,000 setting up my business and releasing my first book, and it took about a year. But thanks to this planning process, I was able to do some research online and create rough estimates for the cost of each service so I could save for the eventual payment.

It's important to identify choices you need to make, and the solution for each, so you can maintain your path once you have committed to it. For instance, I set aside $5,000 for marketing because not a single person had heard of me as an author. If I was going to sell something, people had to know about it. I also spent about $1,000 on a professional website and $1,500 setting up a company properly. For those counting, that's half my budget going to things that were not my books.

If I had not made these choices, I would not have been able to capitalise on opportunities that presented themselves later, such as this book. However, if I hadn't had $7,500 to spare, I would have had to cut back on my marketing, my webpage, or even sacrifice the quality of my book.

Making choices is inevitable. The worst thing you can do is to make no choice at all because you fear making the wrong one. A wrong choice will always teach you something if you look hard enough. This means you can avoid doing it again in the future. Doing nothing is also a choice, but it's one that gets you nowhere.

Always make a choice.

ACTION

Sit down with a friend or a family member and critically analyse the steps you have listed to achieve your COG.

Write down any choices you identify as you go.

Once you have finished analysing the list, begin finding solutions to the choices you have identified.

We have all the steps, but what does it look like in action?

Zoe is a Year Nine girl who has a head full of plans and no idea what to do with them. Let's help her break them down.

Zoe's goals:

1. Win Gold at the State athletics competition for the 100m sprint
2. Beat her friend at Fortnite
3. Win Gold at the Olympics for gymnastics
4. Win Gold at the Olympics for judo
5. Become a physiotherapist for the Adelaide Crows (Australian Football Team)
6. Learn all the Taylor Swift songs on guitar
7. Go bungee jumping

8. Buy a car

9. See the Grand Canyon

10. Learn to speak French.

Let's leave it at ten.

Zoe sits down with her parents and talks through her goals. They quickly point out that there are quite a few competing physical goals – judo, gymnastics and sprinting. If Zoe tries to do all of them, she won't have the required skills to succeed in any of them. Zoe decides judo is most important to her.

CENTRE OF GRAVITY 1:
WIN GOLD AT THE OLYMPICS FOR JUDO

After looking at the rest of her goals, she realises that learning is important to her. She has listed: physiotherapist for the Adelaide Crows, learning guitar songs, learning to speak French. She decides to focus on working towards being a physiotherapist for the Adelaide Crows.

CENTRE OF GRAVITY 2:
BECOME A PHYSIOTHERAPIST FOR THE ADELAIDE CROWS

The last few are a bit of an odd mix: beat her friend at Fortnite, go bungee jumping, buy a car, see the Grand Canyon. Of the four, three require money. As she does not have a job and wants to spend her spare time focusing on judo and physiotherapy study, these are not attainable right now. So she settles on beating her friend at Fortnite.

CENTRE OF GRAVITY 3:
BEAT HER FRIEND AT FORTNITE

Now we have our COGs.

Let's pick COG 2 and create a plan.

Choices

Before Zoe even begins looking at the required grades for a physiotherapist, she is faced with a choice. Is she happy to move interstate to study? Or does she want to stay in Adelaide?

She decides to stay in Adelaide, as she wants to train with the Adelaide Crows and her family is in Adelaide. This immediately shrinks her university choices down to three.

Zoe then goes to the website for each university and looks at the ATAR required for each university, and which subjects are required for entry. She discovers the ATAR is between 73 and 88, and while there are no required prerequisites, a SACE 2 knowledge of biology and physics is assumed.

With this information, she ensures she takes physics and biology in Years 10, 11 and 12. She also takes maths studies as it is a requirement for physics. To progress her judo, she takes on health studies for Years 10, 11 and 12; she also takes English in Years 10, 11 and 12 so she has the required skills to structure her essays at university.

As you can see, simply knowing where she wanted to go allowed Zoe to begin working towards it. Once she identified her COG, she was able to eliminate all the other paths and select only the one that will get her where she wants to go.

The power of planning is removing choices you shouldn't need to consider, before you waste energy on doing so.

A common COG is to get a certain grade in a specific subject. One thing that comes up in all schools and across all topics, is writing essays.

Essays all follow a similar structure.

Here are the steps to complete an essay using the COG method:

- *First, start with the end in mind: get an A on the essay.*
- *Next, break the essay down into who, what, when and how.*
- *Who is the essay meant for? Write down which teacher it is for.*
- *What is the essay about? Write down the topic for the essay.*
- *When is the essay due? Write down the date and time.*

- *How is the essay formatted? Write down any specific requirements of the essay (Times New Roman, 12pt, double-spaced, number of words, or pages, etc)*

Now you have the basics out of the way, it is time to break down the essay itself.

Identify any areas you need to research. Write these down in a list, then start to work through them with the following questions in mind:

- *Who is it about? Write down the country, people etc that the essay is focused on.*
- *What is it about? Write down the specific focus of the essay.*
- *Where is set? Is the essay set on a specific place or time?*
- *Why did the thing happen? What is the history leading up to the incident/thing?*
- *When did this happen? Note any specific dates or times which are important in the essay.*
- *What happened? How did it happen?*

Once you have collated all the information required, it's simply a matter of putting it all together. If you do not have an essay template, ask your teacher for one. Failing this, you usually can't go wrong with an introduction, a body and a conclusion:

- **Introduction:** Background and thesis.
- **Body:** A paragraph outlining each point you want to make.
- **Conclusion:** Restate the thesis, and leave your conclusion regarding the thesis and information provided.

No matter how large the essay, this format will always be applicable.

Your final COG plan looks like this:

- Get an A
- Edit essay
- Write conclusion
- Write points
- Write background
- Write thesis
- Identify points
- Conduct research
- Understand the essay
- *Set dates for each of the required readings, then* begin to work your way through them.

Something else that occurs in almost every school subject is an exam.

Exams are a hated pastime of mine. However, you can prepare for them just as well as you can for an essay:

COG: Get an A on a maths exam.

Answer the following questions:

- *What is the exam covering? This should be the topics you have studied throughout the term.*
- *Where is the exam being held? Write the specific location of the exam.*
- *When is the exam? Write the date and time of the exam.*

Exams are easier to prepare for than an essay, as there will be a specific list of things you need to understand in order to pass. Simply list all the topics you have covered, and you will see what you need to study.

- *Look at your list of topics and identify any that are strengths. If you do not feel that you need to study them, remove them from the list.*
- *Now add specific dates for studying the weaker topics.*
- *Add in a specific day to write a cheat sheet if you are allowed.*

Your COG list looks like this:

- Sit the exam
- Write cheat sheet
- Study topic C
- Study topic B
- Study topic A
- Create study timetable
- Ask a buddy to study
- Identify strengths and weaknesses
- Get study topics from teacher/syllabus

The power of this approach is that you don't study everything. You focus your time and energy on your weakest points and bring them up to scratch.

Note that *you do not need to do all of this alone. Most students dread exams, and the best way to attack most problems is with the support of your peers.*

With your list of strengths and weaknesses in hand, approach your friends and ask for a study partner. Make sure you don't pick someone you know you won't study with. Just because someone is fun, doesn't mean they are a good study partner.

We have now walked through COG theory from start to finish.

It sums up to this:

1. Write down all your goals.

2. Sort them into themes.

3. Pick three COG's, ensuring no more than one from each theme.

4. Create a list of actions, working back from the COG to where you are now.

5. Find a mentor.

6. Ignore every other goal you listed.

7. Succeed.

You have the tools now.

Use them.

Yours in service,

Michael Ball

www.ingramcontent.com/pod-product-compliance
Lightning Source LLC
Chambersburg PA
CBHW022043050726
47591CB00003B/922